One in heaven who sympathizes with us. We can come boldly to the throne of grace to beseech Him.

In heaven, there is One who sympathizes with us and has mercy on us; He feels our burden. He will make our burden light. At times, friends on earth may lighten our burden, but this Friend in heaven is always ready to bear our burden. He not only bears our burden in feeling, but in reality as well. He sympathizes with us, and He is gracious to us. It is as though we are the only ones He loves. He is only concerned about our affairs. He is such a Lord! Thank and praise God! We have such a Lord!

From *The Collected Works of Watchman Nee*, Set 1, Vol. 18, pp. 295-299.

WATCHMAN NEE

The SINNERS' Friend

LIVING STREAM MINISTRY
Anaheim, California • www.lsm.org

© 2001 Living Stream Ministry

All rights reserved. No part of this work may be reproduced or transmitted in any form or by any means—graphic, electronic, or mechanical, including photocopying, recording, or information storage and retrieval systems—without written permission from the publisher.

ISBN 0-7363-1207-2

Living Stream Ministry
2431 W. La Palma Ave., Anaheim, CA 92801
P. O. Box 2121, Anaheim, CA 92814 USA

03 04 05 / 10 9 8 7 6 5 4 3 2

---

fully sympathetic towards others. Every time He sympathized with others, His heart was like a piece of clean paper on which any letter or drawing could be inscribed. Praise and thank the Lord that His heart was empty and wholly reserved for others.

He not only sympathized with the people of that time, He also sympathizes with us today. He is our High Priest, and today He sympathizes with us in heaven. What He experienced was a thousand times harder than what we experience. We can trust in Him and pray to Him. Whatever difficulty we have, He joins Himself to our feelings. He is gracious to us, and He helps us. He will bring us peace.

Hebrews 4:16 says, "Come forward with boldness to the throne of grace that we may receive mercy and find grace for timely help."

Many times we feel that others do not consider our problems to be important and that no one can sympathize with us, comfort us, or help us. At these times, we surely feel how heavy our burden is and how much our suffering is. But there is

THE SINNERS' FRIEND

When the Lord Jesus was on earth, He was tempted in all things. He felt pain when He suffered; He felt sorrow when He was misunderstood. He experienced a great deal of suffering and encountered many persecutions. When He experienced these temptations, He had the same feelings as we do. Therefore, He can sympathize with our weaknesses.

The Lord sympathized with man's weaknesses, but He never sympathized with sin. The Lord Jesus was tempted in all respects like us, yet without sin. He never said, "I sympathize with your sins; therefore, I forgive you." He sympathized with the weakness of man's flesh. What is the weakness of the flesh? It is the weakness in our soul. He sympathizes with this kind of weakness. When we suffer in the flesh, our soul feels uncomfortable. The Lord can sympathize with this kind of discomfort.

For the Lord to express sympathy

not do is more marvelous and meaningful than what He did. When He was hungry, He did not turn the stones into bread. When He was taken by the enemy, He did not ask the Father to protect Him with twelve legions of angels. His heart was not occupied with His own affairs. He was never preoccupied with His own affairs so that He could not sympathize with others.

Many times when we have our own burdens and sufferings, we have no heart for the sufferings of others. But this was not the Lord's way. If He had been only concerned with the suffering He was about to experience on the cross, He would have been occupied with His own suffering every day. He would not have been able to sympathize with others. If He had thought all the time about His suffering—how it was the greatest and hardest of all sufferings—He would not have been able to care for and help others.

But the Lord lived as if nothing was going to happen. When He met the sick, He healed them. When He met the poor, He preached the gospel to them. He acted as if nothing was going to happen. He was means that He feels what we feel. Do we ever feel what others feel? Have we ever sympathized with others? Many times we can help others, but not have sympathy for them. We do not feel others' sufferings. When we see them in want, we can render them material help. But we have never felt the suffering in their life. When we see a sick person, we can give him food and clothing and serve him. But we may not feel his pain. Outwardly, there may be the grace, but inwardly, there is no sympathy. This means that we do not feel what he feels.

The Lord is the Lord of grace; He is also the Lord of sympathy. The Bible has two titles for the Lord: the sinners' Savior and the sinners' Friend (Matt. 11:19). The title *Savior* speaks of His redemption of sinners, and the title *Friend* speaks of His communication with sinners. He can feel all the pain and sufferings of sinners. Thank and praise the Lord. The Lord Jesus is not only the sinners' Savior, but also the sinners' Friend! Here we see a little of the riches of His glory. Sometimes we may encounter difficulties. Sometimes

The Lord was able to sympathize with everyone while He was on the earth because He not only had the experience, but He also had the love. Once when the Lord came down from a mountain, a leper worshipped Him and said, "If You are willing, You can cleanse me." Immediately, the Lord touched him with His hand and said, "I am willing; be cleansed!" (Matt. 8:1-3). There was a place in His heart for the leper. He could feel the suffering of the leper. Therefore, He touched him. The Lord did not merely have the experience; He also had a heart full of love.

Experience and love alone are not enough. The third thing you need is to not be occupied with your own affairs. This means that nothing occupies you beforehand. Many times a man's heart is occupied with something already; therefore, his heart is closed. As a result, he cannot sympathize with others. He may say, "I cannot even bear my own burden. How can I sympathize with others?"

When the Lord was on the earth, He bore a particular characteristic: He put aside His own needs. What our Lord did

We know that our Lord came to the earth to die. If it were us, we would have thought that since our mission was to die, order to experience the bitter taste of human life and sympathize with man's weaknesses. His thirty-three years of human living and His preaching during the three years were not only to accomplish His mission and work, but also for the sake of sympathizing with us. He had to do this before He could sympathize with our weaknesses.

If there is a broken or wounded heart here today, the Lord is right now feeling what you feel. He knows your afflictions. Not only does He have the grace to save you, but He has a heart that sympathizes with you and feels your feelings.

In order to sympathize with others, experience is not enough. The second thing one needs is love. Some people suffer illness for many years; they are sick every three days and rest every two days. They have tasted the bitterness of their illness, but they still cannot sympathize with the sick patients in the world. They can only sympathize with those they love. They have the experience, but they do not necessarily have love. Consequently, they cannot sympathize with everyone.

we may be lonely. Many people may give us a bad face; many voices may cause us sorrow. Everything around us may seem gray. But we have to know that when the billows roll over us, the Lord is not just our Savior; He is also our Friend! He feels the suffering that we feel. He sympathizes with us and goes through our experiences together with us.

Sympathy was a characteristic of the Lord when He was on earth. The Bible records many examples of the Lord sympathizing with men. He sympathized with the sick and healed them. He sympathized with the hungry and fed the five thousand and the four thousand with the loaves. He heard the cry, "Son of David, have mercy on me," and He healed the blind. When He saw the grief of those whose relative had died, He resurrected the dead. If our hearts are open, we will see the Lord's sympathy poured out upon us. Before He was the sinners' Savior, He was the sinners' Friend.

We know that our Lord came to the earth to die. If it were us, we would have thought that since our mission was to die, all we would have to do is go through our ordained death. We would not worry about anything else. But our Lord was not like this. Although the cross was in front of Him, before His time had come, while He was on His way to death, He sympathized with those whom He met and who had need of Him. Oh what a loving Lord He is!

If anyone wants to sympathize with others, three things are indispensable: the first is experience. In order to sympathize with others, one must first have the experience. If you are in sound health and have never been sick, you will not be able to sympathize with sick patients. If you have never experienced a toothache, you cannot sympathize with those who suffer from a toothache. If you have never had a headache, you cannot feel the pain of those who suffer from headaches. If you have never experienced a certain suffering, you cannot share the feelings of those who experience such suffering. Therefore, you cannot sympathize with them. Experience is necessary; it helps one to sympathize with others.

A sister once said, "I have many things which are hard to overcome and many things in which I have failed. Eventually, I sought help from those believers who were better than I. But they did not understand my problem. It seems that they were born 'holy persons,' and they had never felt the annoyance of failures." This shows that a person without experience cannot sympathize with others.

Why did our Lord not descend from heaven as a grown-up? Why did He have to come through a virgin's womb? Why did He have to be nursed, nurtured, and grow gradually? Why did He have to pass through thirty-three years of suffering on this earth? Why was He not crucified three days after He was born on the earth to accomplish His work of redemption?

Oh, the reason He was willing to submit to all kinds of limitation and suffer every affliction was that He wanted to sympathize with us. He learned the principles of human living. He was misunderstood and persecuted. He was stripped, mistreated, and forsaken by people.

Eventually, He was crucified on the cross. He endured all these sufferings in